This is our planet Earth. It's surrounded by a blanket of gases called the atmosphere. This keeps our planet warm, trapping heat from the sun like a greenhouse.

the atmosphere

heat from the sun

Don't just wait for grown ups to act, it's our world too! We can all do something now to fight climate change.

Planet Patrol

Mick Manning
and Brita Granström

FRANKLIN WATTS

Freya

I was so cross about global warming that I've formed my own group to do something about it. We're called the Planet Patrol. We began as mates at school - but now we've made a website and people are forming 'Planet Patrols' all over the world! To join the Planet Patrol you just have to want to help to defend our Earth against global warming.

First I'll tell you what global warming is, then I'll introduce you to some Planet Patrol members around the world.

Without this 'greenhouse effect' we would all freeze, but now pollution in the air is trapping too much heat. Our Earth is getting warmer and the climate is changing. It's putting our Earth in danger - and all the animals in it.

Planet Patrol Facts

The atmosphere is made up of a mixture of gases including the heat trappers, carbon dioxide and methane! People are adding more of them to the atmosphere in lots of ways.

We burn fossil fuels, such as coal, in power stations to make electricity. This gives off carbon dioxide.

We make things in factories using lots of energy and burning more fuel. More carbon dioxide ...

We travel by car, lorry, train and ...

plane, whose engines burn petrol or diesel fuel ...
even more carbon dioxide!

We dump rubbish which rots and gives off methane gas.

Clara

I live in France. I joined the Planet Patrol to help barn owls. Now I walk to school every day to use less petrol. I have even persuaded my dad to make his deliveries with a horse and cart instead of the old van. So he's in 'the gang' too!

Thanks, Clara!

Sometimes I get a lift to school! How cool is that?

It's been so wet, owls can't always find enough food for their chicks!

Warmer temperatures caused by climate change increase the amount of water in the air — and this leads to more rain. Wetter summer weather keeps voles in their holes — and prevents barn owls hunting properly so they can't feed all their chicks.

7

Kim

I'm from Korea; I joined the Planet Patrol because I love polar bears. I'm saving energy to try and stop their ice caps from melting.

Save Energy! Switch off the lights when you're not using them.

SAVE ENERGY! NEVER LEAVE ELECTRICAL EQUIPMENT ON 'STANDBY'.

Thanks, Kim!

Save Energy! Don't heat your home so much. Wear an extra jumper if you feel cold!

Earth's supply of frozen water is stored in the Arctic and Antarctic but as the sea warms up these ice caps are beginning to melt. Polar bears need the Arctic sea-ice to hunt across.

Max I'm from England and I joined the Planet Patrol because the local newts and frogs were dying out. There weren't enough wet places anymore in this neighbourhood - so I'm making them a pond!

Croak! (That's frog for thanks!)

Despite the extra rainfall in some parts of the world, in other places global warming is causing less rain and more heat. This dries up ponds and bogs — the natural home of frogs, toads and newts.

Aurelia I'm from Italy. I'm so sad that puffins can't find enough food due to global warming. Too much energy is wasted making materials that can be recycled like paper, plastic and glass.

Recycle your household waste!

Sand eel numbers have crashed due to global warming. They are the main food supply for many seabirds like terns and puffins and their numbers are now declining fast, too.

Recycling materials helps fight global warming. It uses a lot less energy than starting from scratch, so a lot less carbon dioxide goes into the atmosphere.

I'd say thank you but my mouth is full!

Che I'm from Brazil. Like all good Planet Patrollers I'm planting a tree. It's crazy that rainforests are being chopped down. It's trees that absorb carbon dioxide from the air!

Plant a tree to help!

14

If every human planted a tree that would be amazing!

The world's rainforests absorb carbon dioxide — lots of it! So why are the forests being chopped down? Well countries that have rainforests — like Brazil and Madagascar — sell the timber and clear forests for quick profit farming. This takes the goodness from the land and the trees can't grow back without help.

Billy Joe

I'm from Australia and our coral reefs are in danger from global warming. Climate change has given us water shortages, too, so I'm saving drinking water. Just a little thing like turning off the tap when you brush your teeth can make a big difference.

As the sea 'warms up' coral reefs are dying. Reefs make sheltered habitats for many important sea creatures to live. Reefs also protect world coastlines from wave damage — the Great Barrier Reef in Australia, for example. Scientists say that coral reefs are disappearing faster than the rainforests.

Millions of us live here!

Gustav I live in Sweden and I just love turtles! Guess what? Turtles are threatened by global warming so I'm shopping locally. Food is imported by air from the other side of the world when we already grow plenty of it here. What a waste of energy!

I am persuading my mum to buy local food.

Water temperatures control how many boy or girl turtles are made. As the water warms up more turtle eggs contain girls rather than boys. This makes it harder for turtles to find mates and make more baby turtles.

Soon there might not be enough boys for all us girls!

Thanks, Gustav.

Buying local food helps cut down on all the fuel burnt by lorries and planes when they take food around the world. Less fuel burnt means less carbon dioxide, and that helps slow global warming.

Hilda

I live in Denmark. I love all sorts of animals but my favourite animals are people! Because of global warming honey bees are dying out, but we all need them to pollinate our crops! As part of Planet Patrol, I'm making compost to cut down on methane.

After six months or so all that gooey kitchen waste turns into lovely, rich soil.

People are animals too! We're all threatened by global warming.

The tiny, disease carrying varroa mite that preys on honey bees is thriving thanks to global warming. In the USA, up to half of all bees are already dead! Bees help feed us all by pollinating the plants we eat.

Household waste rots underground in landfill sites and gives off methane, a powerful 'greenhouse gas'. Composting cuts down on the amount of household waste going to landfill.

Ben I live in Kenya. Global warming has begun to harm our wildlife, so me and my mates have been re-using junk to make our toys. It's a great way to cut down on waste and re-using doesn't burn any fuel.

It's good fun, try it yourself!

Global warming is making much of Africa drier. As water supplies dry up many of its animals are forced to look for new feeding grounds and leave their nature reserves. This gets them into trouble with humans when they eat crops or attack livestock.

Hey, Ben! Can I have a go?

I re-use a lot of my rubbish!

Ali

I live in India and I've persuaded my dad to get involved in building our village a wind turbine. It's clean power and renewable too!

Jenny

I live in Holland and love albatrosses. They're being affected by climate change which has made the weather around the South Pole more stormy.

I'm helping by getting more people to join the Planet Patrol.

Visit our website!

26

Albatrosses don't breed until they are 12 years old and then they only lay one egg every two years. The increasingly stormy weather caused by global warming is disturbing their breeding grounds and making it harder for these beautiful birds to breed successfully.

Find out more. Log on to www.theplanetpatrol.com

Join US!

We can all patrol our planet. Here are some things you can do to help:

Take showers, not baths.

Walk to school.

Re-use things.

Plant trees.

Recycle rubbish.

Turn off your lights.

Shop locally.

Start a compost bin.

Use wind power.

Join Planet Patrol!

Useful words

Atmosphere The mixture of different gases that surround our planet like a blanket. This mixture of gases is the air we breathe!

Carbon dioxide A heat-trapping gas in the atmosphere. Plants take in carbon dioxide to make their food; humans and other animals breathe out carbon dioxide. Burning fossil fuels makes carbon dioxide, too.

Climate The weather patterns in a place over a long period of time.

Compost A mixture of food and garden waste which rots down and is added to the soil to help plants grow.

Coral reef A rocky underwater barrier made up of the skeletons of dead and living coral (a tiny animal).

Energy A supply of power to make things work. Our bodies get energy from food; a car gets its energy from petrol.

Fossil fuels Coal, natural gas and oil are all fossil fuels. They are made from the fossilised remains of plants and animals that died millions of years ago. We burn fossil fuels for energy. Once they are burnt, we can't replace them.

Global warming How our planet is getting warmer and changing its climate. It's caused by pollution in the atmosphere trapping too much heat.

Greenhouse effect The way our planet is kept warm by the atmosphere trapping heat from the sun, in the same way glass traps heat in a greenhouse.

Habitats Different places, such as forests and rivers, where animals live.

Landfill site A large hole in the ground where rubbish is buried.

Mate An animal's partner. It can also mean 'to make babies'. We also use it to describe a friend.

Methane A heat trapping gas in the atmosphere. Methane is given out when things rot and also when cows fart!

Nature reserves Areas of land where wild animals and their habitats are protected.

Petrol The fuel that we make from oil that we use to power some car and motorbike engines.

Pollinate Moving pollen from one flower to another so that a plant can make seeds to grow into new plants. Some plants are pollinated by the wind, some by insects, such as bees, moving pollen.

Rainforests Vast forests that grow mainly around our planet's equator. The trees in them take in a lot of carbon dioxide as they make their food in their leaves.

Recycle To process materials that have already been used to make something useful, such as more of the same material. For example, old paper can be recycled to make new paper.

Renewable energy Energy that will not run out, such as heat from the sun or that made by the movement of wind or water.

Re-using Using something again instead of throwing it away.

Wind turbines Machines that make electricity when the wind turns their blades.

Join
the Planet Patrol by
visiting this website:

www.theplanetpatrol.com

On it you will find out more information about global warming and how you can fight it. You can exchange ideas with other Planet Patrollers and find some fun activities. Sign up and get a free Planet Patrol badge.

Index

For Holy Trinity Eco Council

This edition published in 2010
by Franklin Watts,
338 Euston Road, London, NW1 3BH

Franklin Watts Australia
Level 17/207 Kent Road,
Sydney, NSW 2000

Text and illustrations © 2009
Mick Manning and Brita Granström

Brita and Mick made the illustrations
for this book
Find out more about Mick and Brita
on www.mickandbrita.com

Editor: Rachel Cooke
Art director: Jonathan Hair

Printed in China
A CIP catalogue
record is available
from the British Library.

Dewey Classification: 363.738'74

ISBN: 978 1 4451 0273 3

Franklin Watts is a division of
Hachette Children's Books,
an Hachette UK company.
www.hachette.co.uk

This book is printed
on paper made from
wood harvested from
forests in a manner
that meets Forest
Stewardship Council
(FSC) standards.